Drawing Bats

How to Draw Bats for the Absolute Beginner

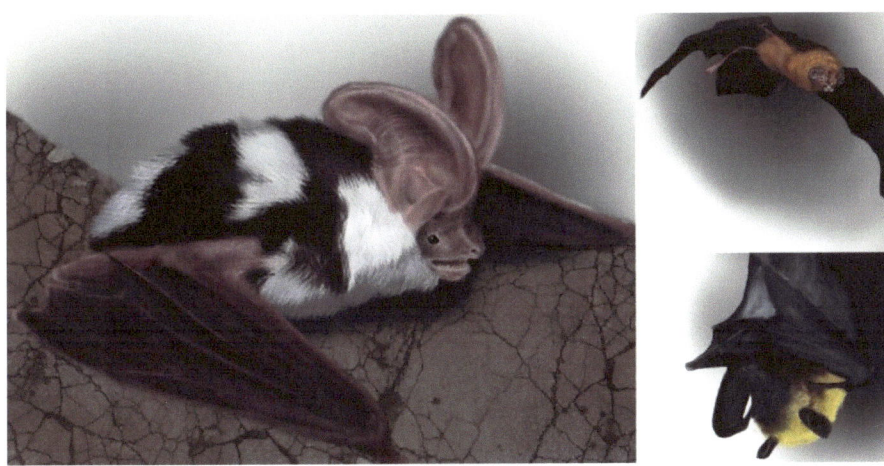

Adrian Sanqui

How to Draw Series

Mendon Cottage Books

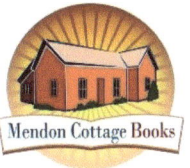

JD-Biz Publishing

Our books are available at

1. Amazon.com
2. Barnes and Noble
3. Itunes
4. Kobo
5. Smashwords
6. Google Play Books

Download Free Books!
http://MendonCottageBooks.com

Table of Contents

Introduction: Drawing a Bat

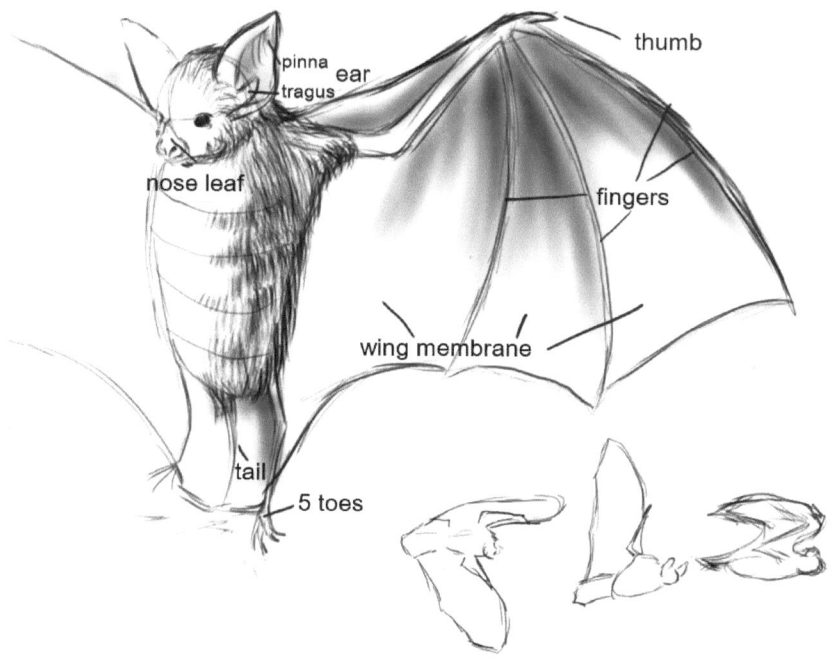

When learning to draw, the first skill one needs to develop is knowing how to follow through the contour planes or dimensions of any basic shape, in order to effectively portray the subject. Observe how the lines travel across the body of the figure and how the depiction of fur (in the case of learning how to draw bats) follows the dimension. How you apply the shade also matters when you want to portray texture. It is also important to know the basic parts of your subject (here a bat) to identify if there is anything missing in your drawing.

The steps in these drawing tutorials are made in a way that can be applied whether you are to draw traditionally or digitally, by starting with a basic shape to create a base, up to elaborating the details.

Drawing tools

Pencils & Charcoals

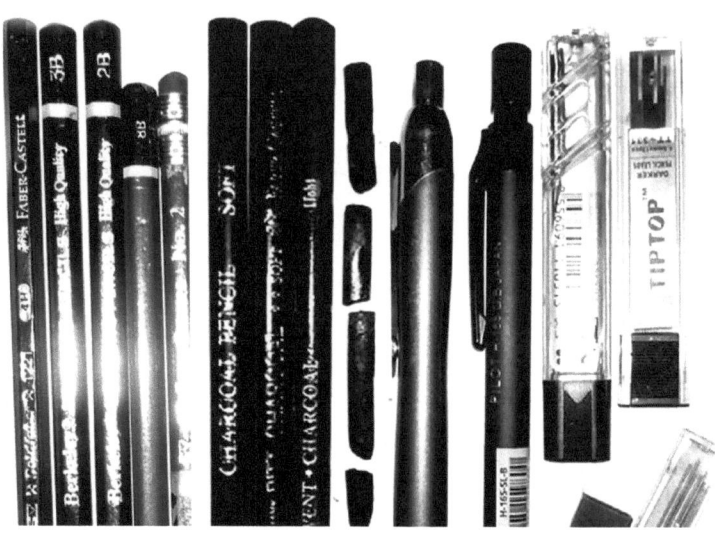

The 'H' engraved near the pencil's tip (side of eraser) stands for "hardness" and it ranges from 2H to 9H. A pencil with only an "H" mark without a number means 1H. The most common type (the one available anywhere) of pencil that does not indicate its grade mark is usually a 2H pencil. The "B" marking of pencils stand for "blackness," this means that they can easily produce darker line marks and are softer than H pencils. It ranges from HB (hard and dark) to 9B (very soft and very dark), so when it comes to B pencils, the higher the number is; the softer and darker it becomes. Different brands have different softness, hardness, and blackness levels, so if you are going to use a certain brand for the first time, you should try them out first before applying it on your main drawing.

Charcoal pencils also come in different grades. The generic grades of soft, medium, and hard are available in different brands. Charcoal pencils are a bit messy to work with; even the 'hard' grade charcoal pencil is still relatively softer compared to those with 4B to 6B grade pencils.

Mechanical pencils are good for small and subtle detailing that requires very thin lines, instead of sharpening your pencil several times just to have a thin and constant fine point. Different grades of lead or graphite is also available for refilling your mechanical pencil.

Erasers & Smudge Tools

Good quality erasers are essential if you are going to use a pencil for drawing. Choose a rubber eraser that is soft and not the ones that leave a faint color or worst a scratch on the paper. Keep them in a pencil case or anything that can protect it from being exposed to the air for too long because some erasers (cheaper ones) dry out and harden when it's left lying around.

A kneadable eraser is very helpful for making highlights and reaching hard to access areas such as the gloss on the eyes or light portions of fingernails and such. It usually looks like a gray slab or a small bar of clay that can be molded or formed to any shape you desire. It doesn't rub off the marking like usual erasers, but instead, it lifts off the graphite from the paper, like absorbing it. Instead of rubbing the eraser with a certain pressure to remove a marking, carefully dab on the portions you want to erase or to simply decrease the applied graphite or charcoal until you recover the brightness (whiteness of the paper) you want.

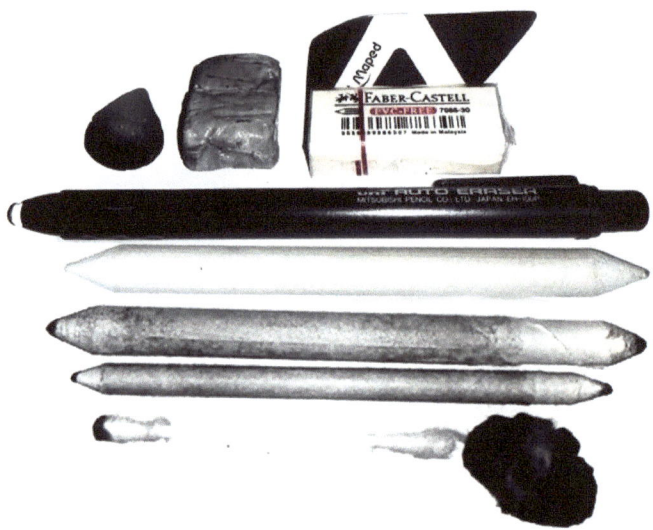

A smudge stick is used for smearing the shades on the portions that are hard to access. Some artists dull down the other tip so it can be used for distributing the shades on the big areas. To avoid ruining the smudge stick, use sand paper to make a blunter tip or to make it even pointier. Smudge sticks or blending stumps comes in different sizes, choose what best fits your needs and it will be a big help for blending gradations.

Keep those used up smudge sticks even if it's already in a rugged state (dirty or worn out), you never know when it might be handy.

Dirty smudge sticks are useful for producing faint shades, and those with torn up tips can make textures that you might find useful.

Coloring Materials

If you are planning to color your drawing, choose a coloring tool that best fits your needs. Oil pastels are good for blending and synchronizing different colors together. It might get messy on your first trials (if you don't want to get messy, just place a clean piece of paper for your palm rest, to avoid rubbing your palm against the colored portions of your drawing) but you'll get the hang of it as you use it more often. Oil pastels are good for beginners as a practicing tool for smearing different color values.

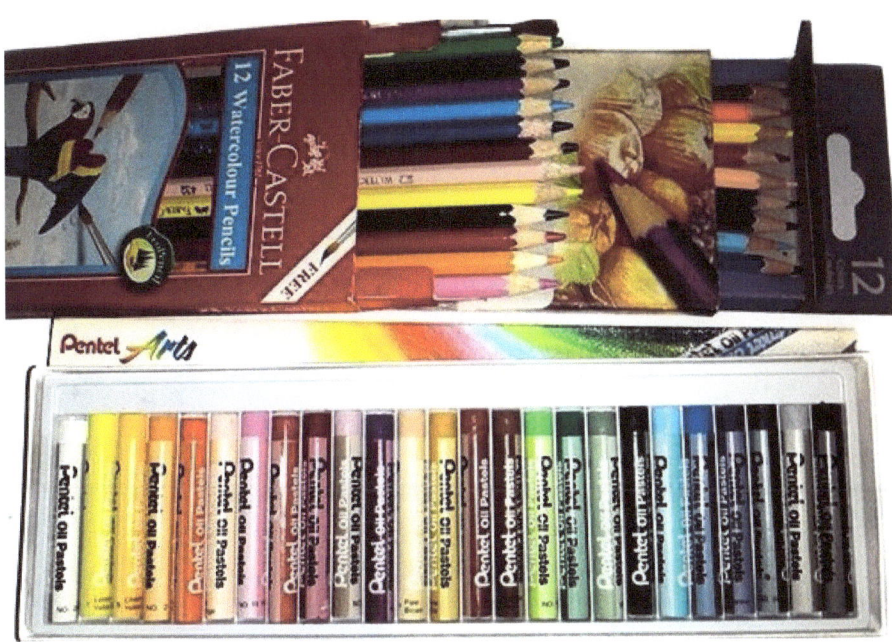

Color pencils are the next best thing for filling your drawing with colored hatches (linear shading), or even coloring via scribbling. This coloring tool is best for small-sized illustrations. Although, the peak of the tone values that a common color pencil set can produce are far weaker than the oil pastel's, and it cannot be smeared (but there are available color pencils which can produce strong color tones just like oil pastel's or even acrylic's, but they are quite pricy; like the prisma color pencils).

Drawing Software

 **Paint Tool Sai**

Paint Tool Sai is known for its light weight performance and speed. This program would easily run even on low-end devices. It has all the essential tools to create illustrations from simple to advance. There are a fair amount of brushes with textures to choose from and it can be adjusted according to your needs.

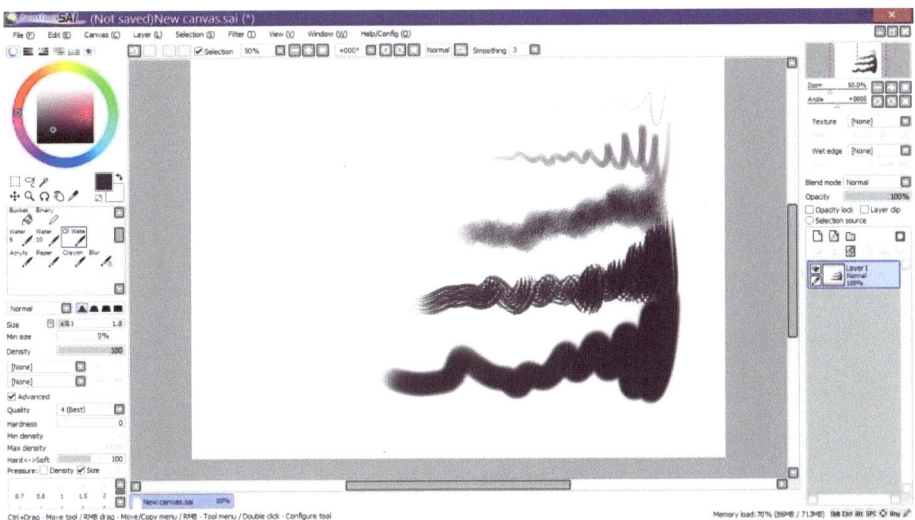

Just like any other app, the lay out of Paint Tool Sai could be intimidating for beginners, with all those features and panels displayed by default, but just play around with it until you get the hang of it and gradually know what the panels and tools are for. Since this software is widely used by a lot of artists, it won't be hard to find tutorials if there is anything you can't figure out on your own. What the users really like about it as a drawing application is it's 'stabilizer' feature which consistently guides your strokes as you make your line work to avoid any unintended squiggles. A feature that is quite helpful and dependable for those who draw illustrations purely digital. It is compatible for pressure sensitivity which is a plus for those using drawing tablets and other units with digitizers.

 **Adobe Photoshop**

Adobe Photoshop is the most popular application used not just by illustrators but also photographers and more, and there's a very good reason for it. The versatility of this software is more than what you need to create a fine masterpiece. From applying effects, textures, and refined adjustments, Adobe Photoshop easily became a 'go to' for professionals and is considered a standard of 'industrial-grade' editing software. The number of brushes in this software by default is already filled with quite a useful variety, and the number of features and effects you may use to enhance your work is laid out in a very organized manner.

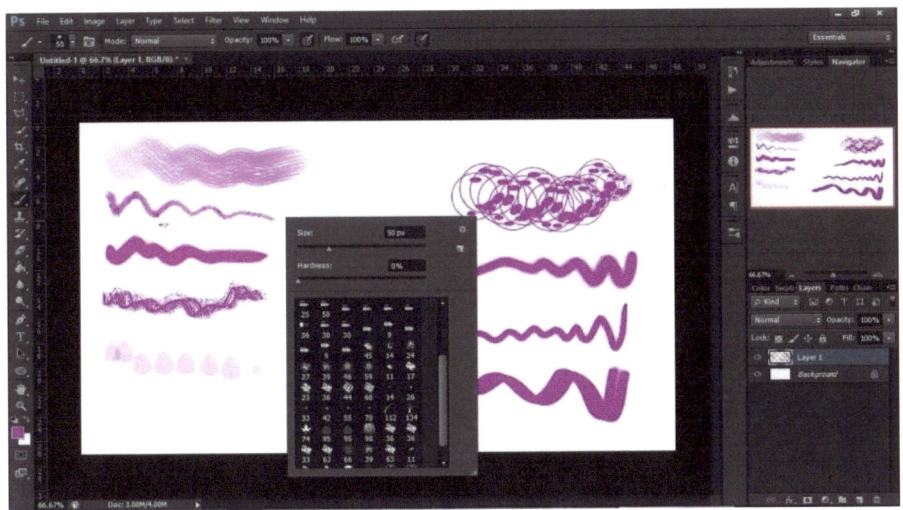

Although versatile with a handful of features, Adobe Photoshop is originally designed as editing software. You might feel a slight difference in drawing directly through the application compared to the likes of Paint Tool Sai which is specifically designed to make digital illustrations. And aside from this small differences in the 'feel' factor, it is quite a heavy application to run. You are going to need a powerful machine to get the most of its efficient performance. For its popularity, Photoshop has been released with different versions and updates. As expected, newer versions have more features than the older versions, but is also more demanding in terms of system requirements.

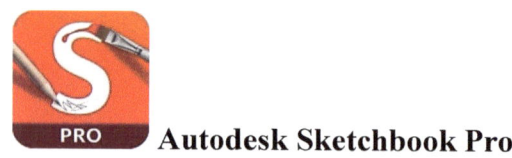 **Autodesk Sketchbook Pro**

Autodesk Sketchbook Pro is probably the most lightweight software that is filled with features that an illustrator would need to make a decent artwork, either just a sketch or a full-blown deeply detailed illustration. It may not be in the same league as the editing capabilities of Adobe Photoshop, but as the name suggest, this software is made to produce digital illustrations and not photo manipulations. With its user-friendly interface and the simplicity of the layout, this drawing application has easily became one of my personal favorites.

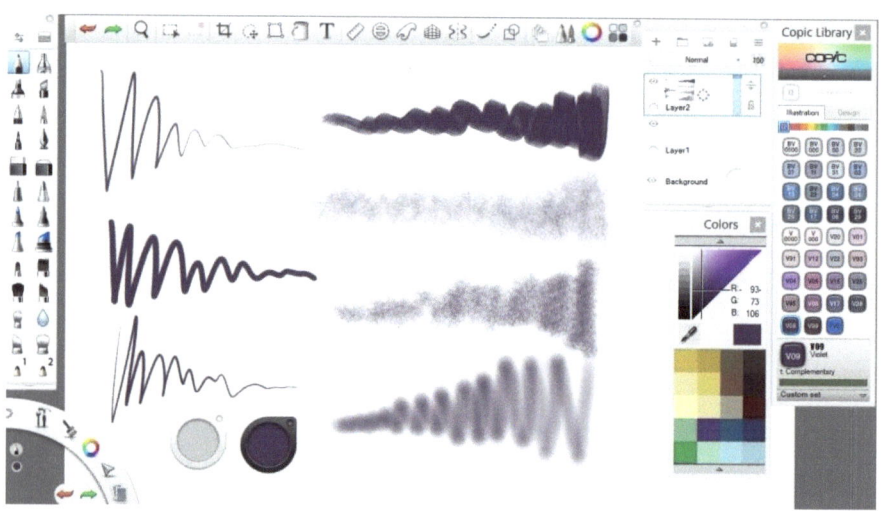

Due to its appealing simplicity and minimal system requirements, Autodesk Sketchbook Pro became popular with beginners and even to some professionals. The common needs of a digital artist are met by this lightweight software like being able to create several layers, opacity adjustments for each one, and pressure sensitivity for using digitizers and tablets. The tools are placed on easily accessible panels and the buttons are adequately big enough to be pressed easily which is somewhat a problem on other applications when you are solely relying on touch rather than keyboard commands. But since the interface is different than most drawing and editing applications, you will have to play with it for a little while so you can get used to it. And unlike Paint Tool Sai and Adobe Photoshop, you can only open one project or file at a time.

Now, that I have covered the basic physical tools and/or digital tools you may choose to use, let's begin actually drawing bats.

Drawing a Bat in Flight

Vampire Bat

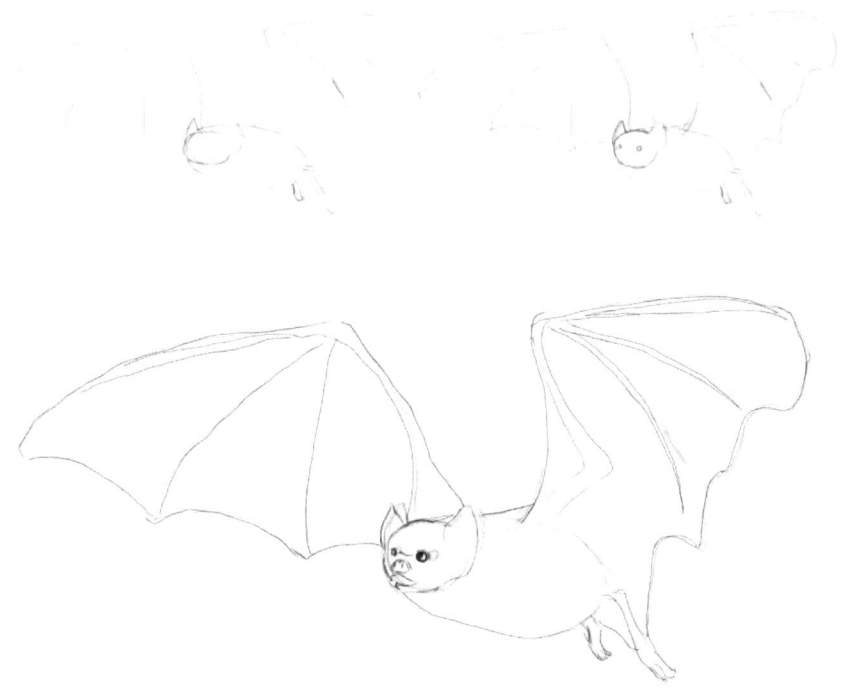

Create a base

Establish the mass of the body using a simple oval base and the head, and then establish thee spans or lengths for the arms/wings using simple curved lines. At this point, it is easy to establish the shape in its view perspective, as the bat is closest to a quarter view angle.

Complete the primary shape of the bat by establishing main features of the shape and the outlines of the limbs including the wings. Put a curve on the lower outlines of the wings until it reaches each finger.

Properly layout the primary outline of the figure

Once the base is complete, use it to properly compose the primary outline of the figure. Define the facial features and the other primary details.

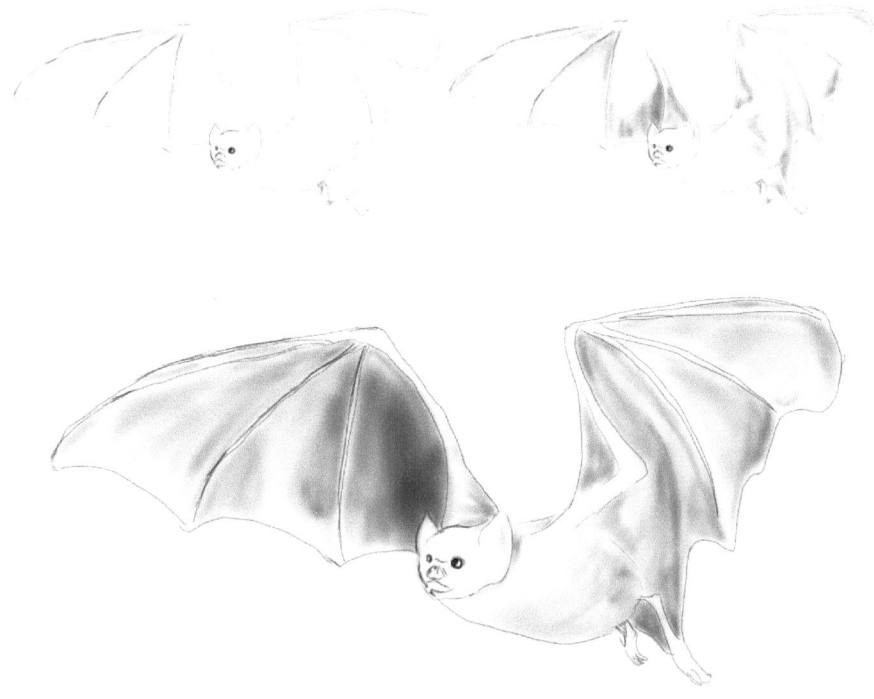

Redefine the main figure with clean outlines and remove the unnecessary sketch marks.

Make some shades to define the depth and shallowness of the planes.

Once the main outline is properly defined and clean, start defining the shallow concaves of the wings with shading. This initial step of applying shades is done to simply serve as a guide to determine the depth or shallowness of the planes, thus, serving as a guide for further shadings.

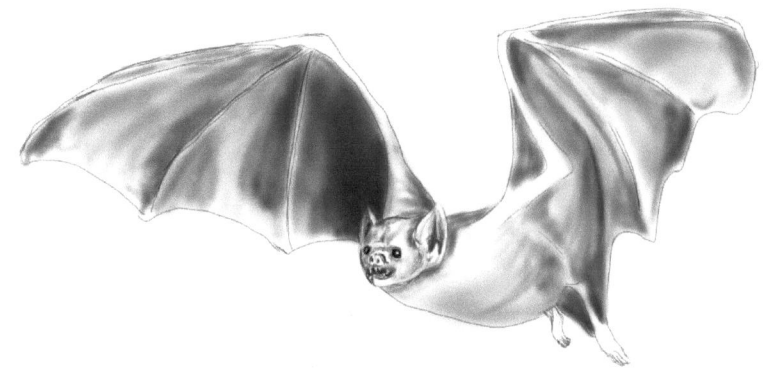

Apply the primary shading of the figure.

Apply a thin toning to the figure by shading most of the portions. Define the contour shape of the figure as you apply the shade. Since some areas were shaded before, they should now appear darker than the applied mid-tone value.

If you are drawing traditionally, remember to constantly smear the shades as you apply another layer, this will get rid of the rough texture of the line strokes and even out the shades within each portion.

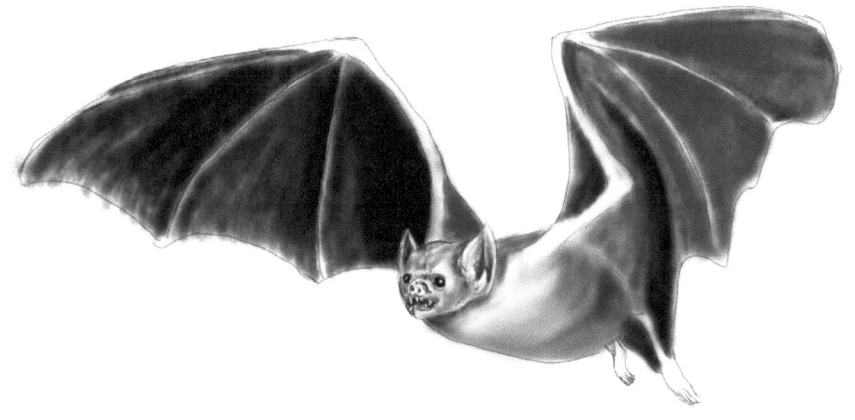

Darken the shades

Once the contour shape of the figure, or the dimensions of the planes, is established, you could now strengthen the dark value of the subject.

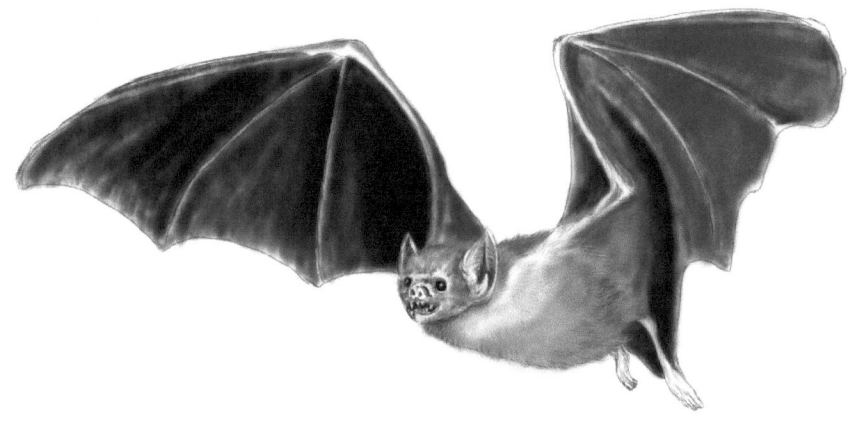

Darken the wings even further

The wings should have the darkest value amongst the figure as this area is practically black in color. Take note of the fingers across the wings: they should be visible, but should not be shaded with the dark tone the wings itself.

If you are drawing with charcoals or lead pencils, it might be difficult to avoid the thin linings/fingers as you apply the thick shade of the wings span especially when you smear. But just like in any case, the tone value could be easily retrieved and fixed with a fine point eraser (bladed eraser or an eraser pencil) or with a kneaded eraser (basically, anything that can get through those very slim areas).

Further increase the dark value. Apply another layer of shading for the last time. Remember that the wings should appear as the darkest part of the figure. Once the tone is set, add more short strokes of fur to thicken the coating.

To effectively portray a texture, dab the planes or areas with used cotton (the one you used to smear the shades). Do this repeatedly on the wings and make some final retouches.

A nose of a vampire bat has a thermoreceptor. It sticks its nose against the skin of its target and detects the nearest blood flow. It usually hunts small preys, but they are also known to attack larger ones when the animal is sleeping and defenseless. Its teeth are short relatively apart from each other, but is sharp enough to penetrate thick skinned animals. Unlike the other bats who simply crawl with their wings and legs folded, a vampire bat is able to adapt and can somehow sprint using its four legs. It can even jump a short distance. Aside from drinking blood, it is also fond of milk.

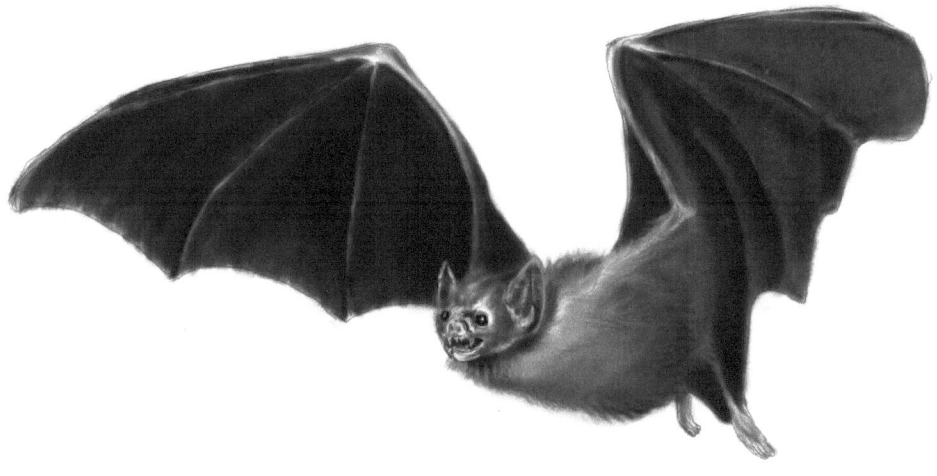

Like most of the other bats, they live and survive in a colony or roost, especially the females. They recognize a family member, and they tend for them when they fail to hunt for food. A common vampire bat usually feeds on land mammals, but there is also a kind that preys on birds.

Ghost-Faced Bat

Define the wing span and the mass of the body

The form of the figure is foreshortened because of its angle. In this particular case, the left wing would appear shorter than the right wing which extends downwards. The base of the trunk/body is also shortened to go with the angle, making the head of the bat face a quarter view.

Establish the other primary details

Using light hand strokes (sketch strokes), define the facial features and form of the wings with its soft slopes on of the each finger gaps. Use the base as a guide to see what portions of the figure overlaps the other.

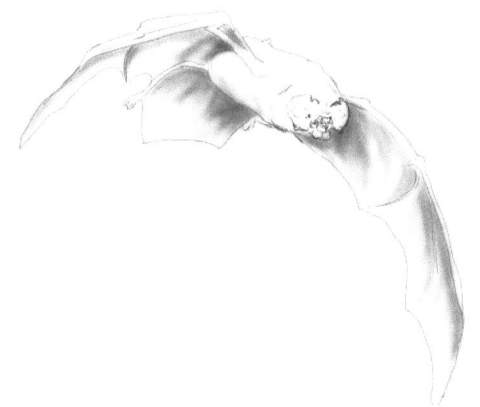

Redefine the primary outlines

Retrace the primary outlines with stronger and smoother line strokes, then erase any unnecessary sketch marks.

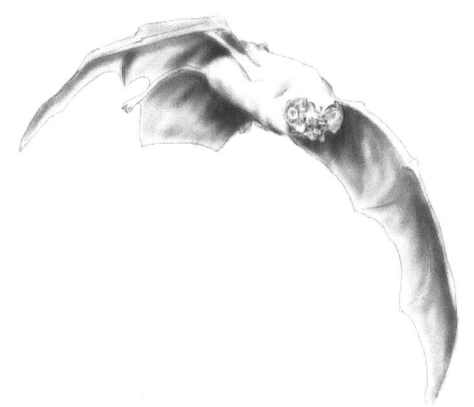

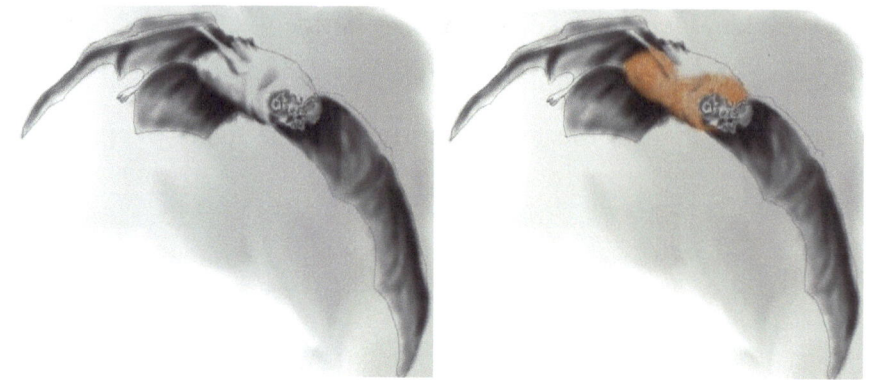

Convey the inner surface of the wings

Establish the shallow concaves and minor ripples of the wings (and tail) by applying shades on its respective areas (darker portions means deeper sections). Smear the shading to smoothen the texture.

Darken the shades

If you are drawing traditionally, lighten your hand strokes as you go back to the previous shading. Then distribute the tone by smudging it to the lighter areas accordingly. If you are drawing digitally, just simply adjust the opacity of the brush and go over the areas that should have a darker tone.

Put a tone or shade value on the background

To get rid of the blankness or whiteness of the paper/canvas, just simply apply a faint shade or tone in the background.

Start defining the fur coat with short consecutive strokes

To effectively portray the short fur coating of the bat, use short and thin line strokes to fill the trunk/body. Since the primary color of the coat is orange, you are going to play with different color values of dirty yellow to reddish brown.

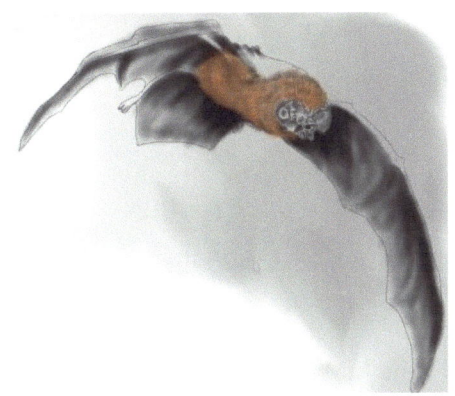

Start with a basic orange, then follow it with brownish orange to obtain a darker value. Use a yellowish orange to portray a brighter tone (tips of the fur and portions that should appear brighter). If you are drawing traditionally, always start with a color with a lighter/brighter value, since it is hard to overlap the dark values with a brighter color. But if you are drawing digitally, all you need to do is gradually adjust the palette to make the orange tone get darker on most parts, and then brighten the tone again to gain back the brighter fur strokes.

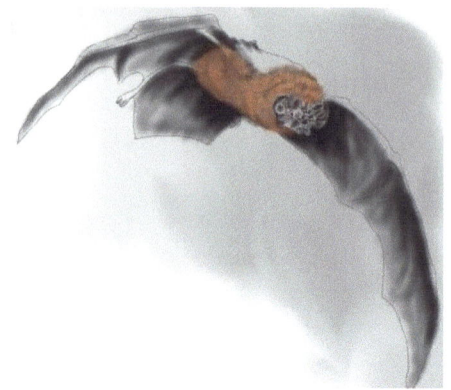

Overlay a dark brown value on the wings

Play with hues of dark brown that would blend with the black value of the wings, and then re-darken it once again with slight touches of black. To achieve a faintly speckled texture if you are drawing traditionally (on paper) dab the areas of the wings with a used cotton (the one you used to smudge the shades) or intentionally sprinkle some excess of a charcoal then press it against the paper. You could also dab a brush (with charcoal stains on it) to achieve this effect. But if you are drawing digitally, it could be as simple as using a textured brush to overlay the areas.

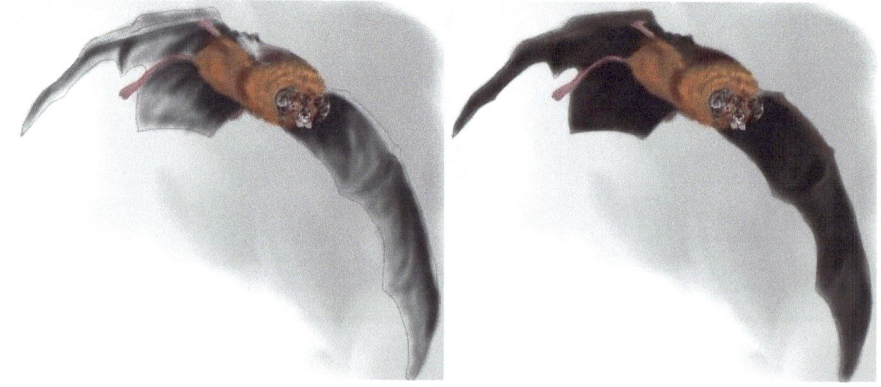

The odd-looking face of this particular kind of bat is a result of its underdeveloped nose and large round ears (the upper potion of its ears meets on its forehead) and a number of its skin flaps or facial protuberances. These unique facial structure is believed to help the bat in picking up sonar vibrations(echolocation). The color of a ghost-faced bat varies from different shades of light orange to dark brown.

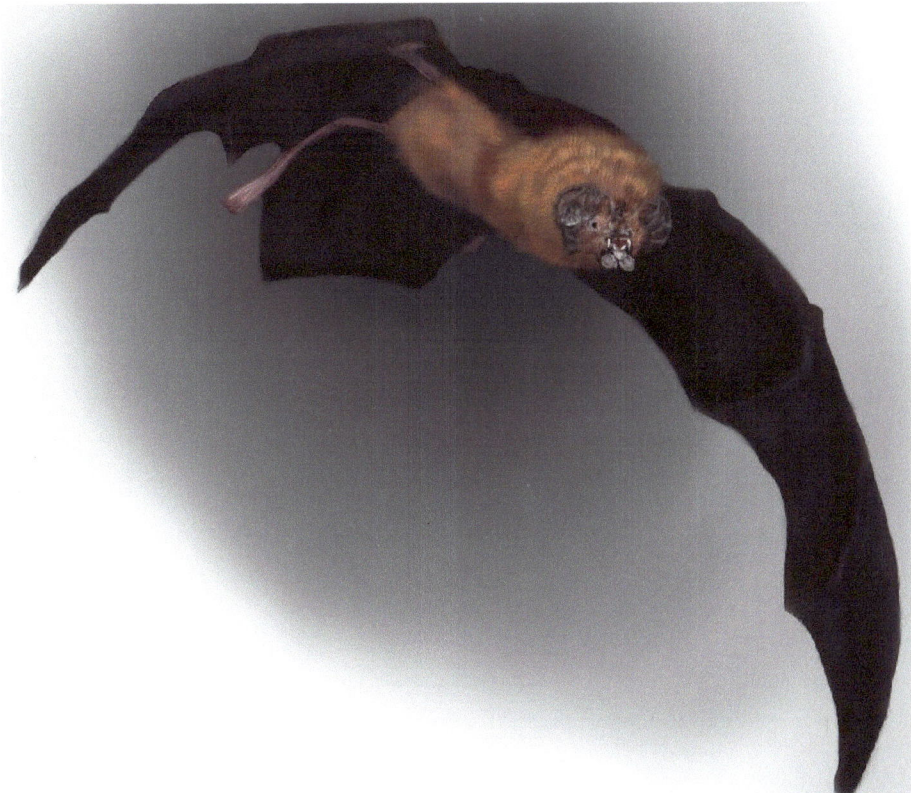

Drawing a Bat at Rest/Hanging

Flying Fox Bat

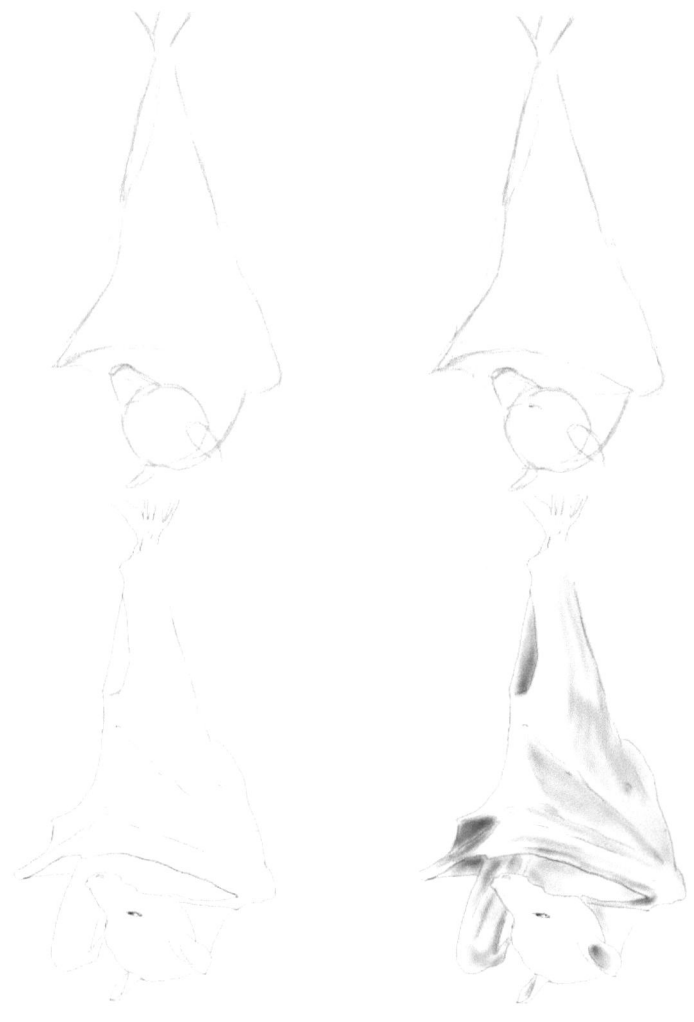

Draw a base for the bat

When in this position, a basic figure of a flying fox bat appears triangular or conical. Using this simple shape makes it easier to define the mass and proportion of the subject. Just add a sphere to establish the size of the head and a curve for the neck.

Make a better outline of the figure with smoother and clean lines
Once the basic base is made to convey the mass and shape, sketch the contour outline of the bat.

When you are satisfied with the sketch, redefine it to establish the primary outline of the bat and convey the other features, and then clean it up by removing the unnecessary line marks or the sketch lines.

Apply the first layer of shading
To depict the dimensions of the figure easily, define it with varying shades. Just simply convey the curves and depressions of the structural planes with faint shading, and then smear it to smoothen the respective areas.

Apply the secondary shading to convey a tone for the entire figure
Once the primary shading that depicts the dimensions are complete, apply another layer of shading that defines the tone or dark value of the figure.

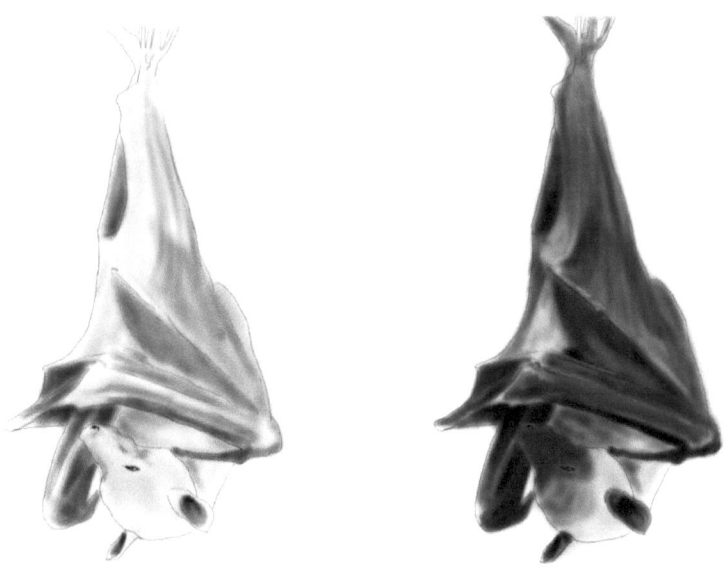

Elaborate on the tone values of the subject

At this point, you have already established the ripples and folds of the figure's planes. Now you can amplify the dark value of the shades and define the particular areas that should appear darker, those that should just be in a mid-tone, and the subtle brighter sides of the planes depending on how it is stretched or folded.

Some shading should also be applied on the head, neck, and chest of the bat before you apply the color. The muzzle and ears should have a dark value. Apply some rows of brushed shades to convey the furry texture of the body.

Apply the color of the trunk/body

Apply the base color first; either you are drawing digitally or on paper. And then use darker tones to convey the furry texture. Once the primary color values are applied, build up the subtle differences of the tones and the other small details necessary.

Keep on building up the tone and apply some texture

If you are drawing traditionally, you could create a slightly rough texture by dabbing a brush or even just by simply running the sides (the blunt or flat sides) of whatever medium you used to apply the color (like a pencil color or dry pastels). This effect will be effective in conveying the texture of the wings' surface.

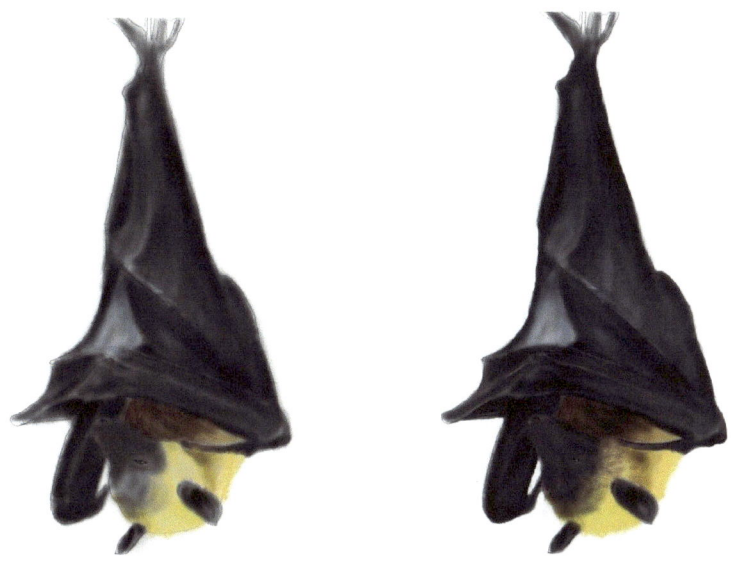

If you are drawing traditionally, you could just easily use a textured brush with low opacity. Use some faint bluish gray color to retrieve some brighter value on the respective areas of the wings, dark gray tone if a color of a certain plane needs to be flattened, and a light gray tone to brightest areas. Do not use white on its highest value as this might create an effect of a glossy surface. And then further elaborate the furry texture of the trunk with consecutive short thin lines that follows its previously depicted flow.

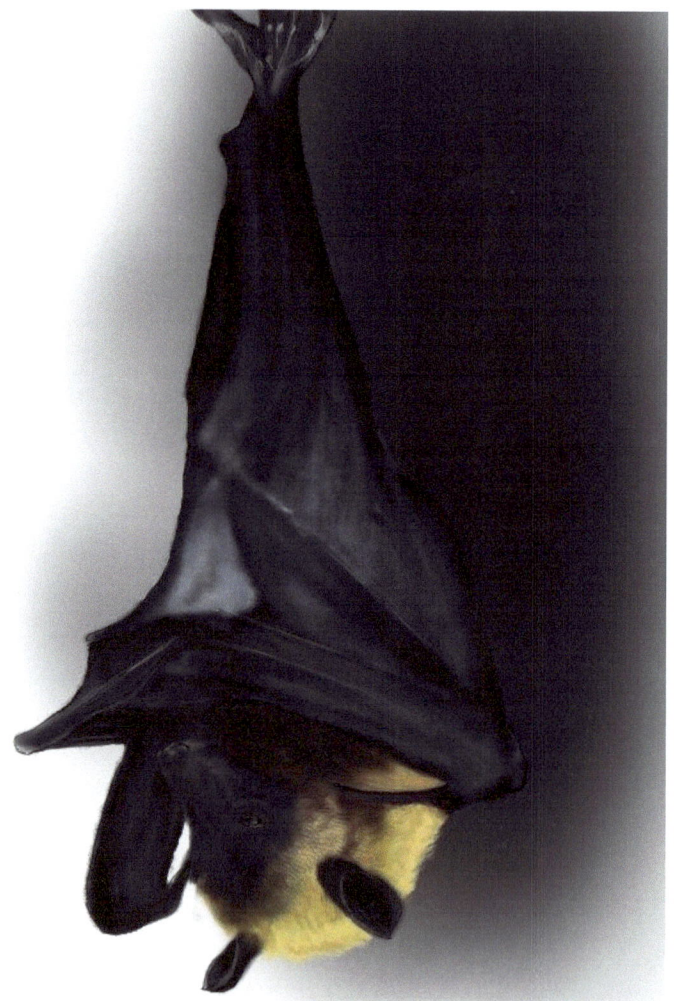

The color of flying fox bats are usually two toned (from black or other darker undertones) but there are also kinds with one solid tone. It varies from light yellowish brown, reddish orange, or brownish copper, and this is combined with darker (usually dark brown to black) dorsal sides. The color values of their fur could change depending on the season and gender. Most kinds of these species are just as big and small as the other bats, but the largest types (megabats) also belong to this family (particularly the great golden-crowned flying fox).

Drawing a Crawling Bat

Spotted Bat

Establish the mass and proportions of the figure

Start with the oval shaped body and a sphere for the head. The folded wings are basically triangular, and the big ears of the spotted bat are basically bean-shaped.

Sketch the shape outline of the bat

To make a better depiction of the bat's figure, use the base you've made to make sure that all parts are properly proportionate.

Re-establish the main outlines

Retrace the primary outlines of the figure with finer line marks, and then remove the sketch lines and any unnecessary markings

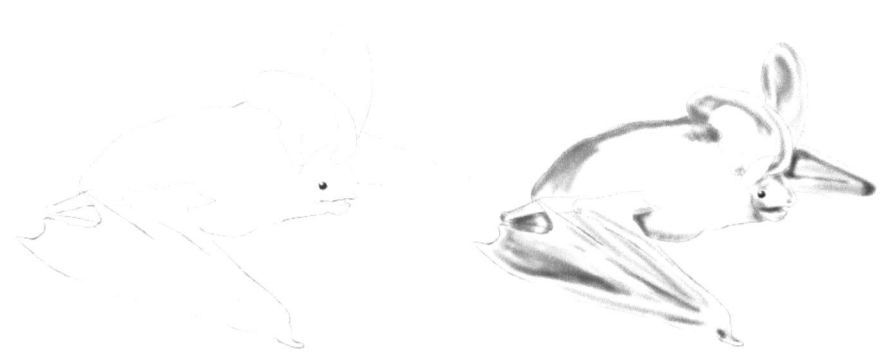

Convey the contour dimensions of the figure by using soft shades

Use shades to define the dimensions of the bat. Convey folds on the wings and the concave dimensions of the ears. These shades would serve as a guide for the next steps and would also appear as portions with noticeable dark tones.

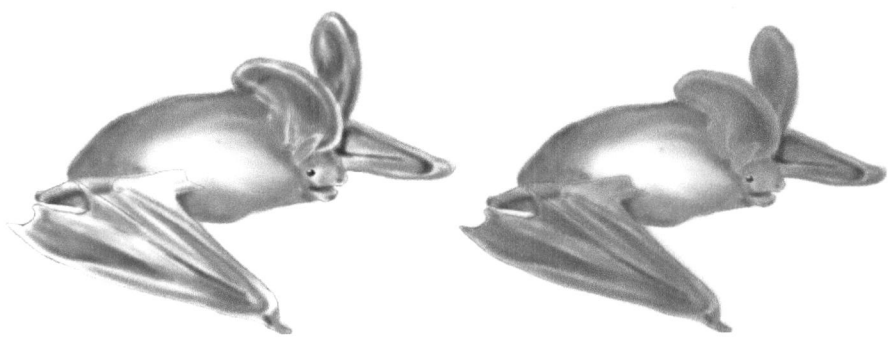

Convey the mid-tones

Make another layer of thin shading to establish a fair tone (not too dark and not too bright). This time, use a light gray to apply a primary toning to the figure. As you shade (since this would be the mid-tone) take note of the portions that should appear brighter according to the figure's contour shape/dimensions.

If you are drawing traditionally, it is easier to do this with a gray charcoal or pastel. This second shading process will darken the previous one you previously made (shades to establish dimensions). Apply the shades with light hand strokes and evenly distribute them to the areas (smear). Don't leave any linear markings as this shading step should not have any visual texture effect. But if you are drawing digitally, simply increase the brightness of the gray color palette and decrease the brush's opacity.

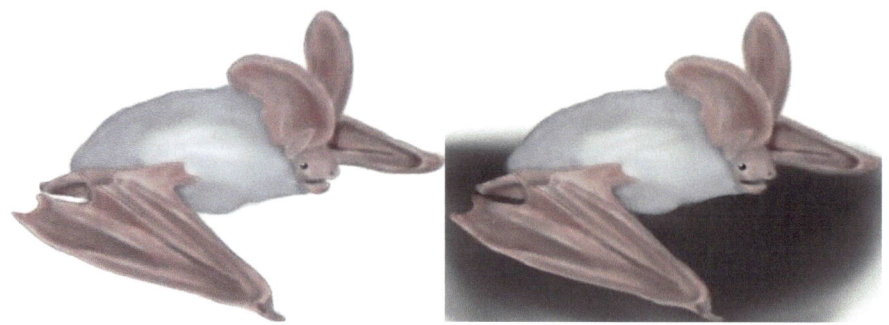

Apply the primary colors of the bat
Start applying the primary colors of the figure. A spotted bat has white body fur and a grayish pink flesh tone. You will be applying the colors with thin or light strokes since the figure already has a mid-tone and shade it in.

Use light hand strokes if you are coloring on a paper. Use less dense paints, or smear the color if you are using pastels. And decrease the opacity of the brush if you are coloring digitally.

Put a tone on the background

You should establish a ground to complete the portrayal of a crawling bat. The main subject should stand out visually, so take note of the figure's tone value and color when choosing a tone for the background.

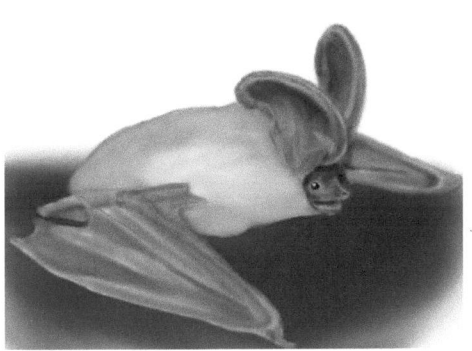

Convey the skin texture

Elaborate the details of the skin texture. The bold skin of the bat has speckles of grayish brown in it. You could effectively portray this by using something that already creates a texture that resembles tiny irregular blots or speckles.

If you are drawing traditionally, the texture can be achieved by using the blunt edges of a pastel or charcoal (preferably a hard kind so it is easier to create breaks on a stroke), or if a brush, dabbing the tip of it with the needed color (washed grayish brown). And if you are drawing digitally, using a textured brush with low opacity would easily do the trick.

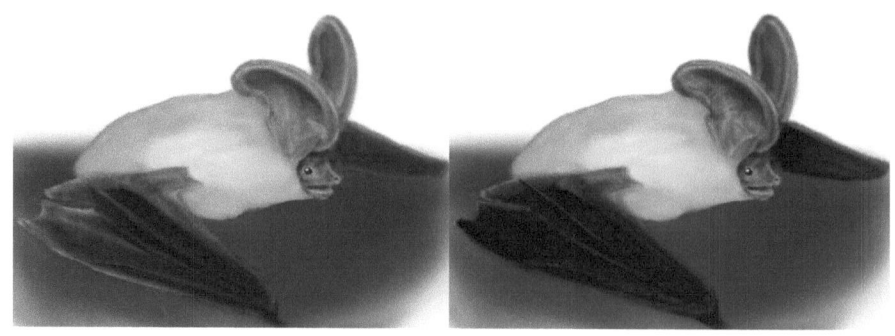

Darken the tone of the wings and convey any other subtle details on the skin

The wings (particularly, the wing membranes) are significantly darker than the other portions of the exposed skin. Darken these portions but take note of the ridges or folds that should appear darker or brighter (basically, you should still follow the pattern of the tone. Just amplify the shading. Again, only use light hand strokes or low opacity brushes.

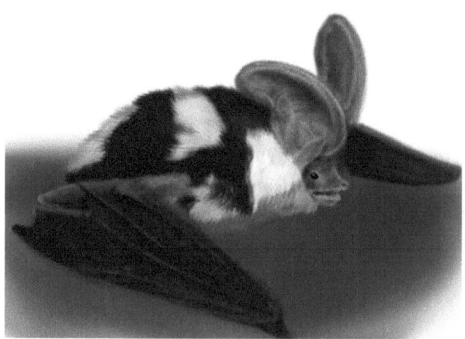

Depict the furry texture of the trunk

Finally, convey the furry texture of the trunk/body with a couple of overlapping layers of consecutive short line strokes. Keep in mind that the white fur coat of the spotted bat (as the names says) has huge black spots on it. Then make the final retouches and work on the subtle details further until you feel satisfied with it.

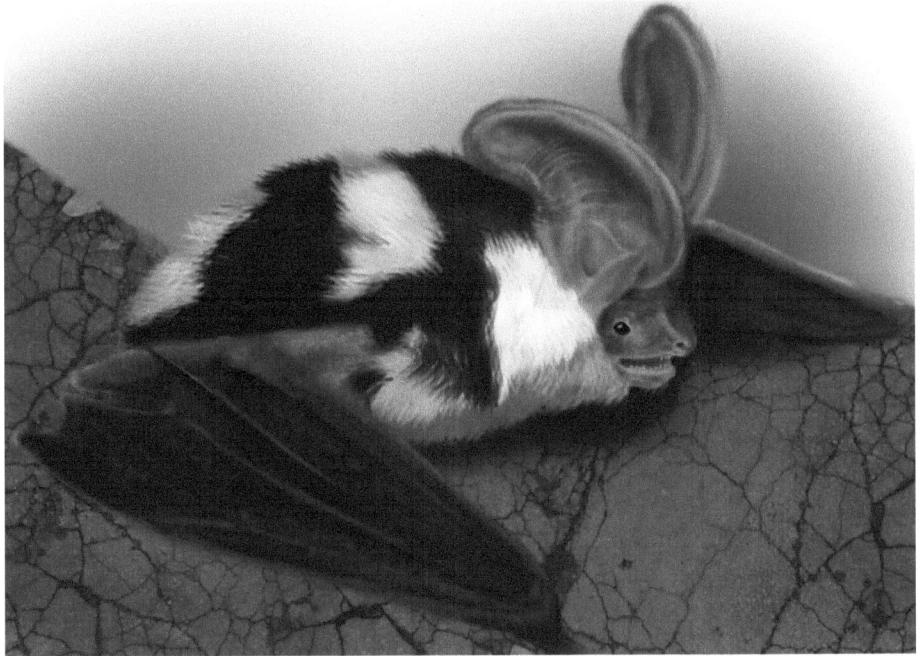

This beautiful bat species belongs to the family of vesper bats (common bats) with a pretty distinct characteristic. It has big long ears that arch backwards when at rest. The ventral side (underbelly) of its trunk/body is covered with short white fur, while the dorsal side is covered with black fur with three white spots. Unlike most bats, the echolocation call of a spotted bat is low, which makes the sound audible for humans.

Drawing Bat Heads

Pocket Free-Tailed Bats

Create a base

Use simple shapes to establish the mass and proportions of the
features. Convey the shape of the head first (it could be a sphere or
pear-shaped in this case) and then depict the facial features.

Sketch the primary outline of the head

Convey the main outlines of the bat's head with more distinctive
visual definitions. The mouth of a pocketed free-tailed bat has a series
of wrinkles or grooves on its lips. Ears and eyes are fairly sized and
the nose is well developed without any skin protuberances.

Retrace the outline

Refine the outlines to make the definite ones more visible. Retrace
them and remove all the sketch markings and any other unnecessary
lines to prepare the figure for shading.

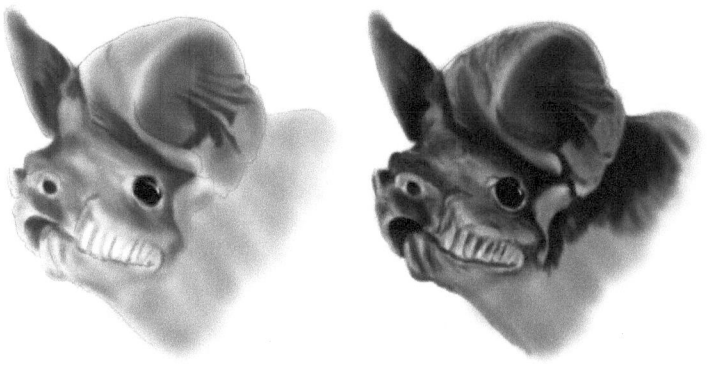

Convey dimensions via shades

Start depicting the tone values of the planes that creates the dimensional features of the subject. Keep it simple at first; the darker areas being the ones with depth or overshadowed by other portions, while the lightest portions are the nearest planes in view. And once the dimensions of the planes are established by the shades, intensify the tones and smear them accordingly to soften and smooth the texture.

Define the subtle details

Elaborate the details, define the other details with subtle shades. Convey the texture of the skin with very faint very small speckles. You could apply this using a tip of a brush or by dabbing a used cotton very lightly (on paper) or a textured brush with low opacity (in digital). For conveying the fur, just simply apply a number of consecutive short lines until you fill the respective area.

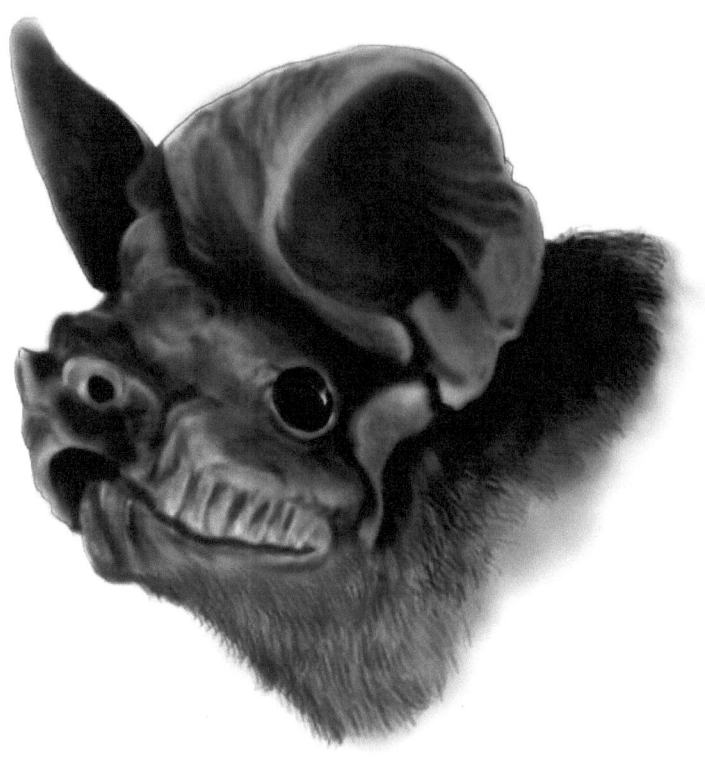

Sword-Nosed Bat

Define the basic shape of the head

To easily convey the proportions of the head, create a sphere for a base and then add the two long ears. You could also easily place the stout muzzle by using the cross reference mark (with it being right below the half of the sphere). In this way, you could then establish the view angle of the head.

Once the base is complete, use it to sketch the actual shape/primary outlines of the bat's head

Define the facial features properly. Draw the distinct details of the nose; the nostrils facing sideways with the small flaps right below it, and the unique sword-shaped protuberance right above (blocking some portions of the face). The sides of its long ears are slightly folding inwards, and the tragus is also significantly long (reaching half of the pinna's length).

Redefine the main outlines with more visible lines

Retrace the sketch you've made with finer line work to properly define the main outlines of the head, and then erase the unnecessary sketch marks.

Apply the primary colors

Aside from the nose having a faint pinkish flesh tone (excluding the nose leaf), a sword-nosed bat basically has a brownish orange fur coat and a deep grayish brown skin tone. So, use orange and brown to apply the primary color value of the bat.

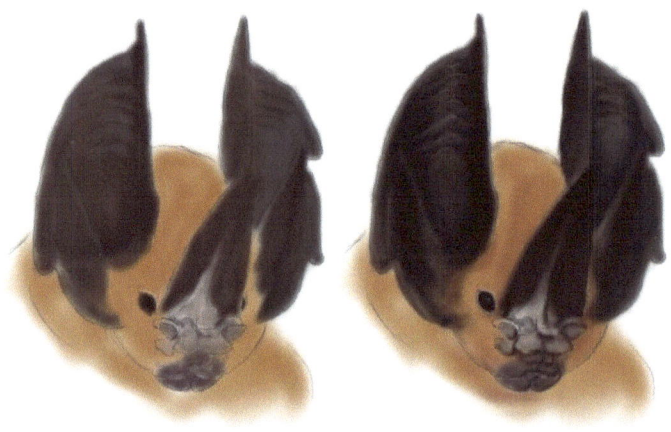

Convey the darker and lighter values of the primary colors

Overlay the primary colors with the same color of a different value. Basically, you put another layer of color over the first one on the areas with a darker or lighter tone (depending on the area) to convey the dimensions of the figure., just convey the values as how you would when you apply the shades to convey the contour shape (farther sides and deeper areas being darker as the nearest planes of the figure gets brighter). Darken the inner edges of the ears to signify the fold and its concave shape, and also darken the far edges of its subtle ridges on the upper side of the pinna. Darken the inner portion of the nose leaf, including the curved edges of the nose.

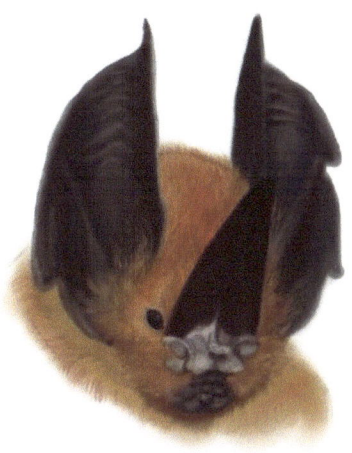

Once you are satisfied with the tone values of the base, convey the fur texture of the bat with short soft lines (once again, with different values). Use different values of the brownish orange, from bright orange to light brown. Remember that the farther sides of the head should be darker, which means that more brownish values should be placed on these areas. And when you are done depicting the fur, finalize the drawing with a faint (either dark gray or black, with a very low opacity or very light strokes) shading to cast shadows and amplify the dark and light values.

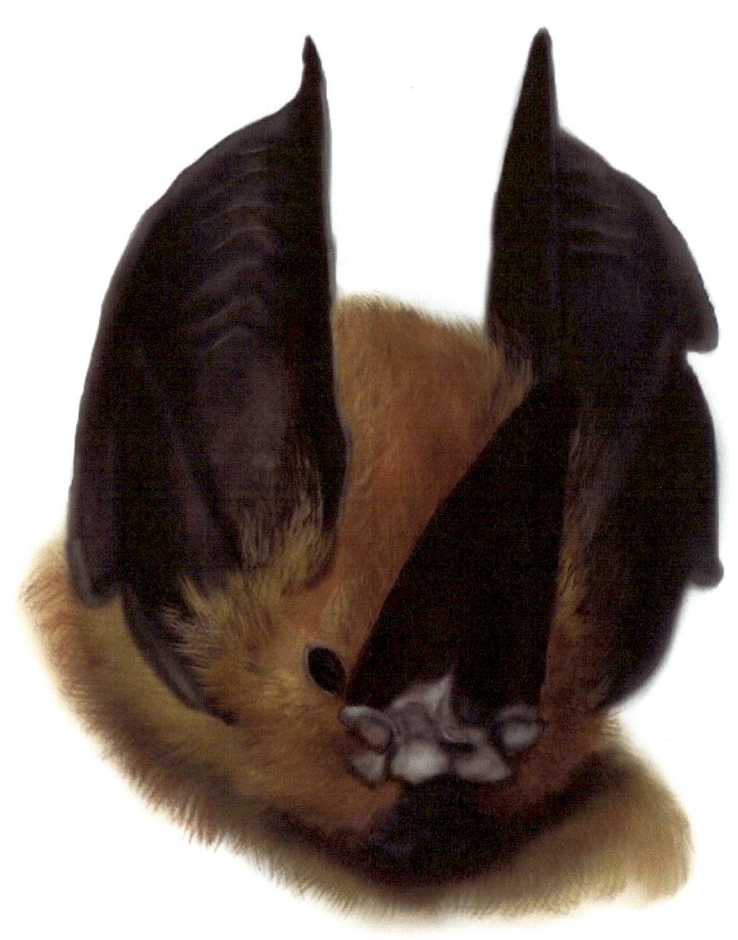

Thank you for reading!

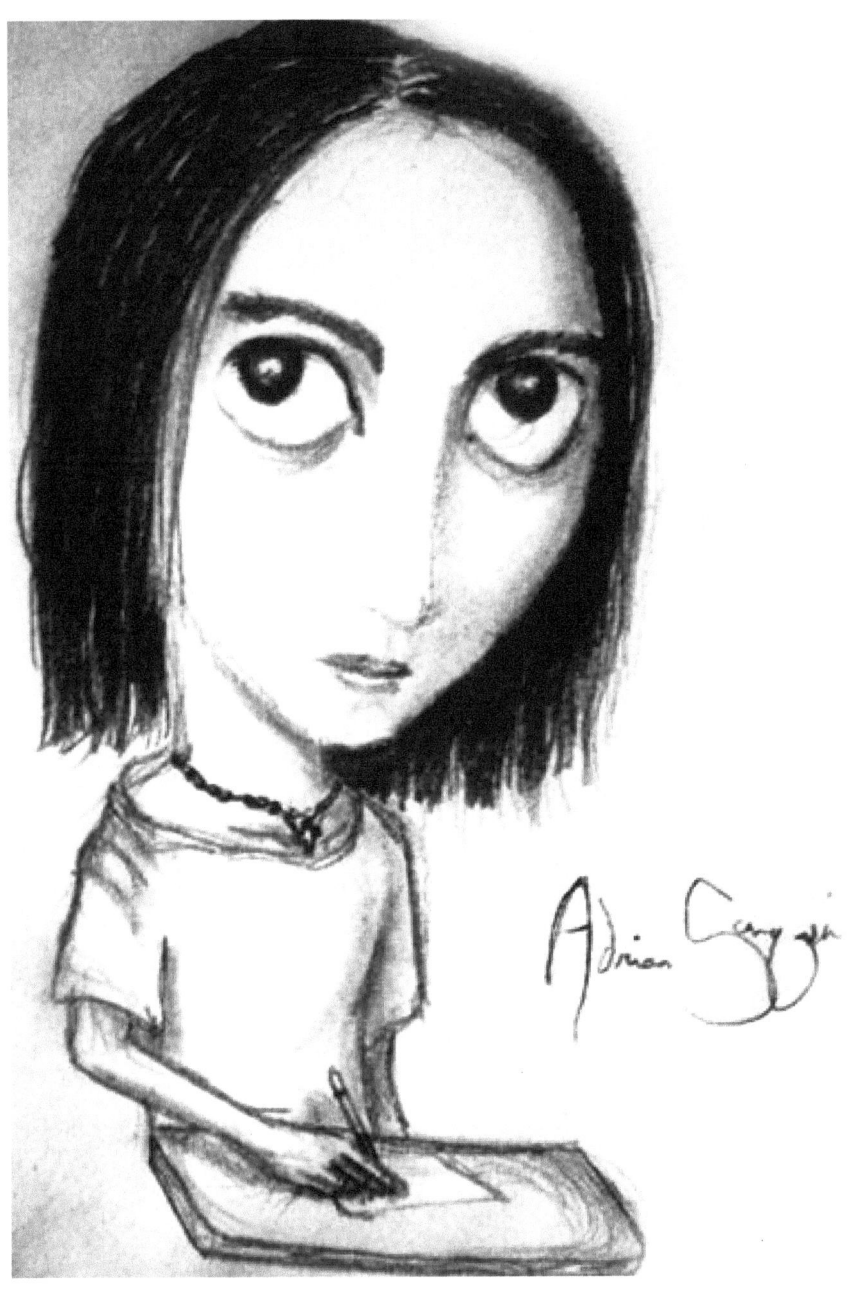

Check out some of the other JD-Biz Publishing books

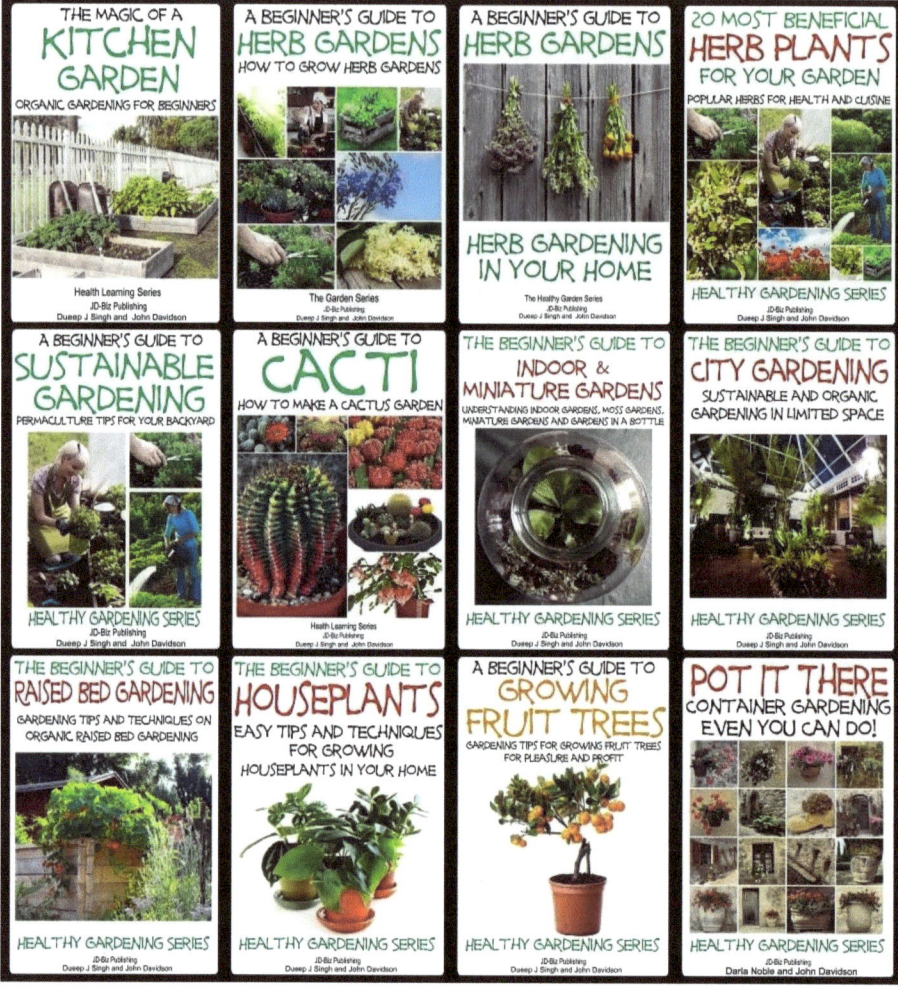

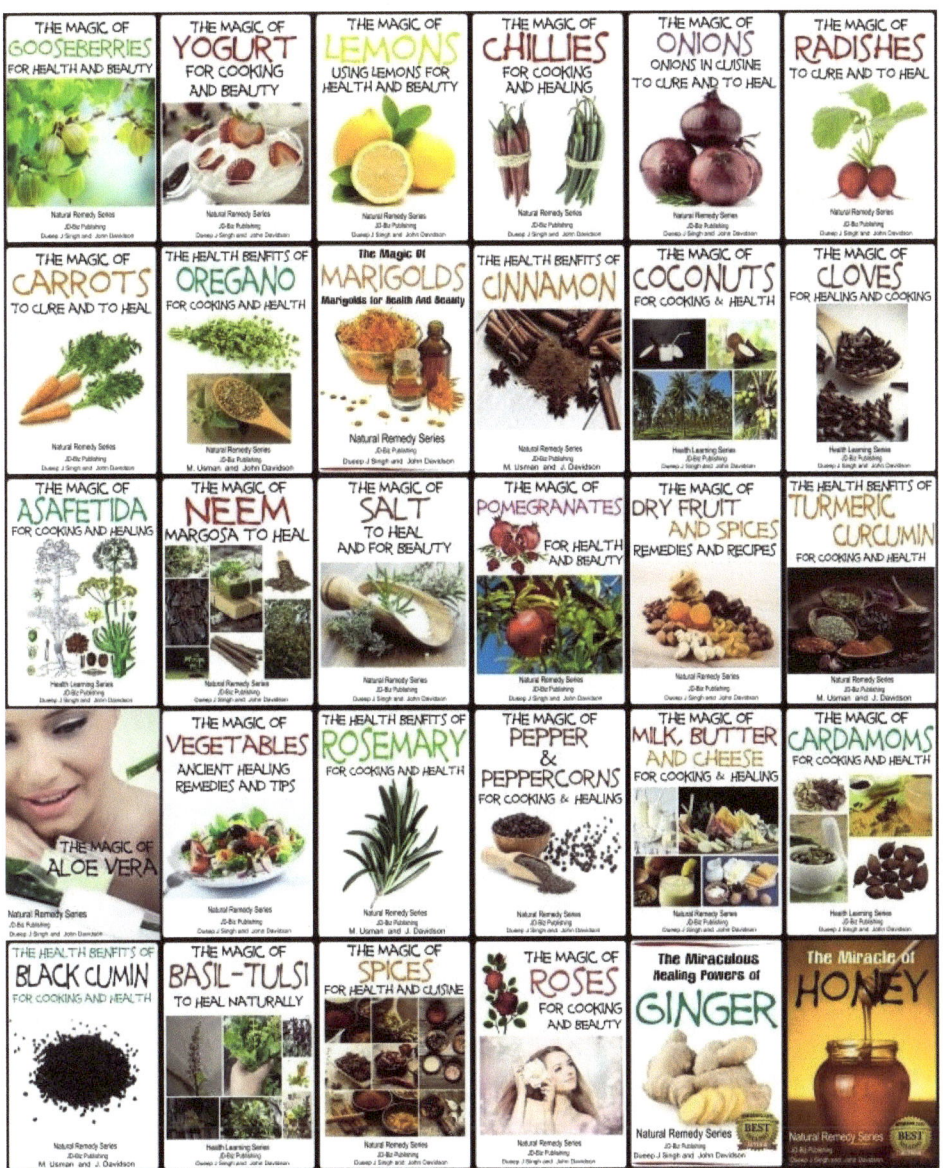

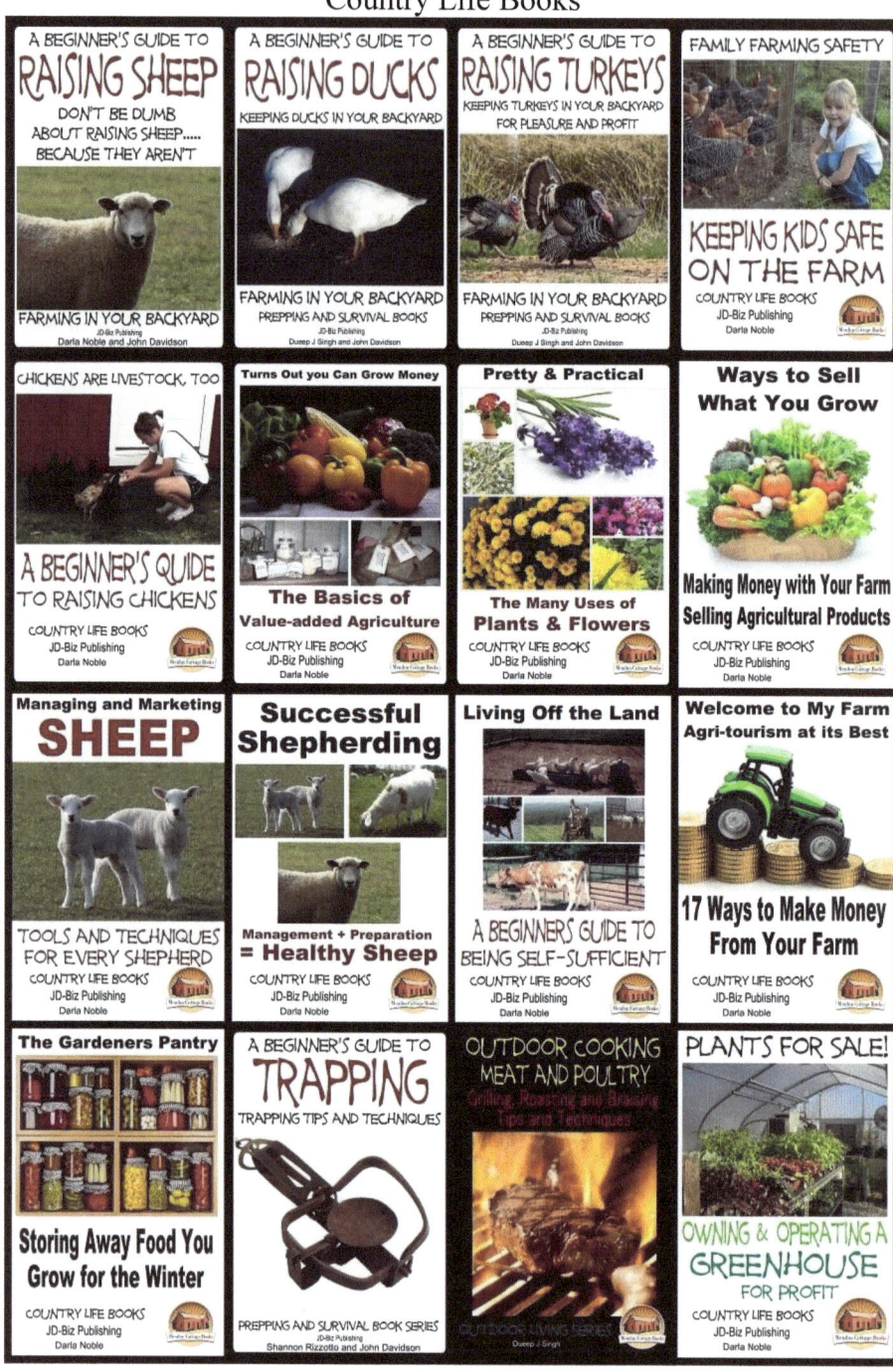

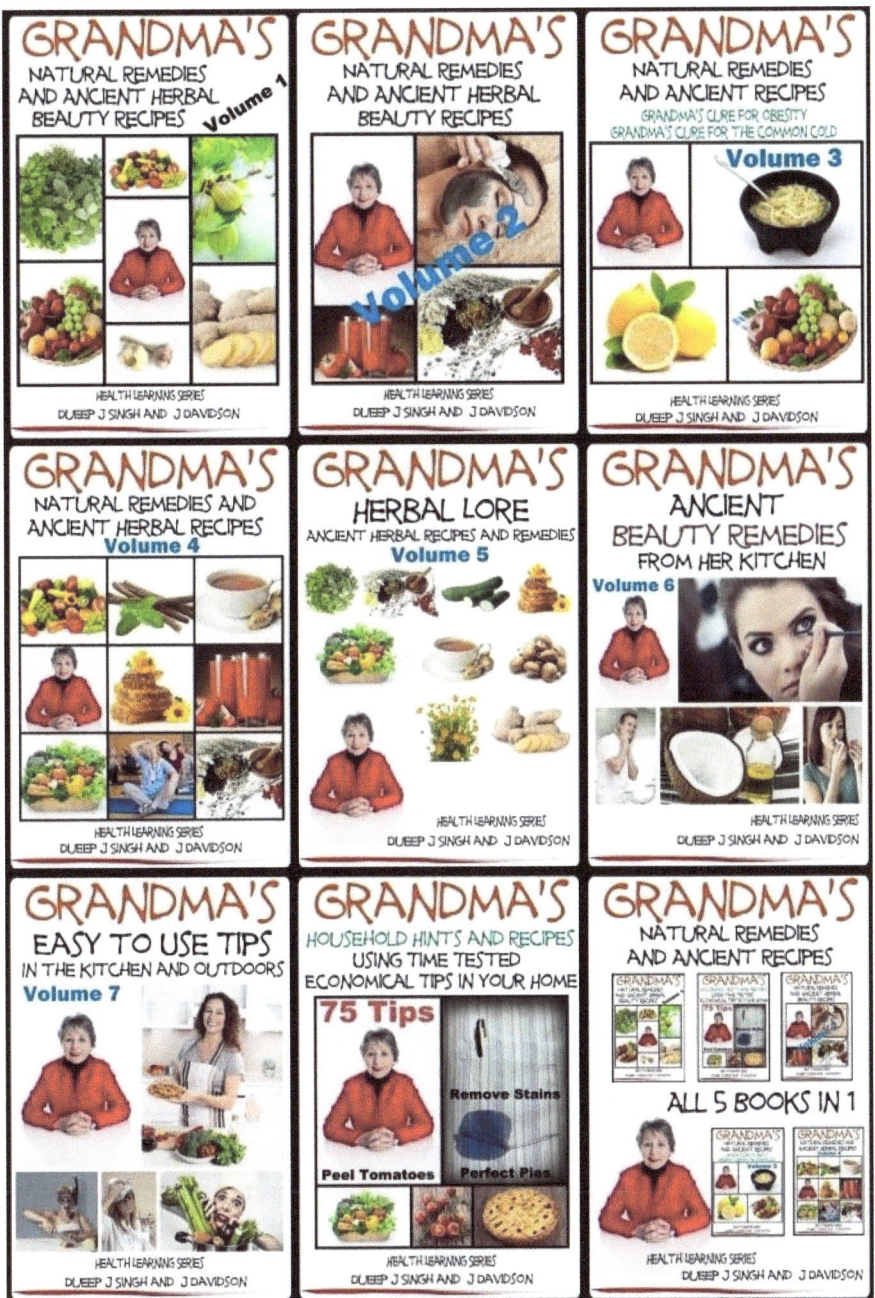

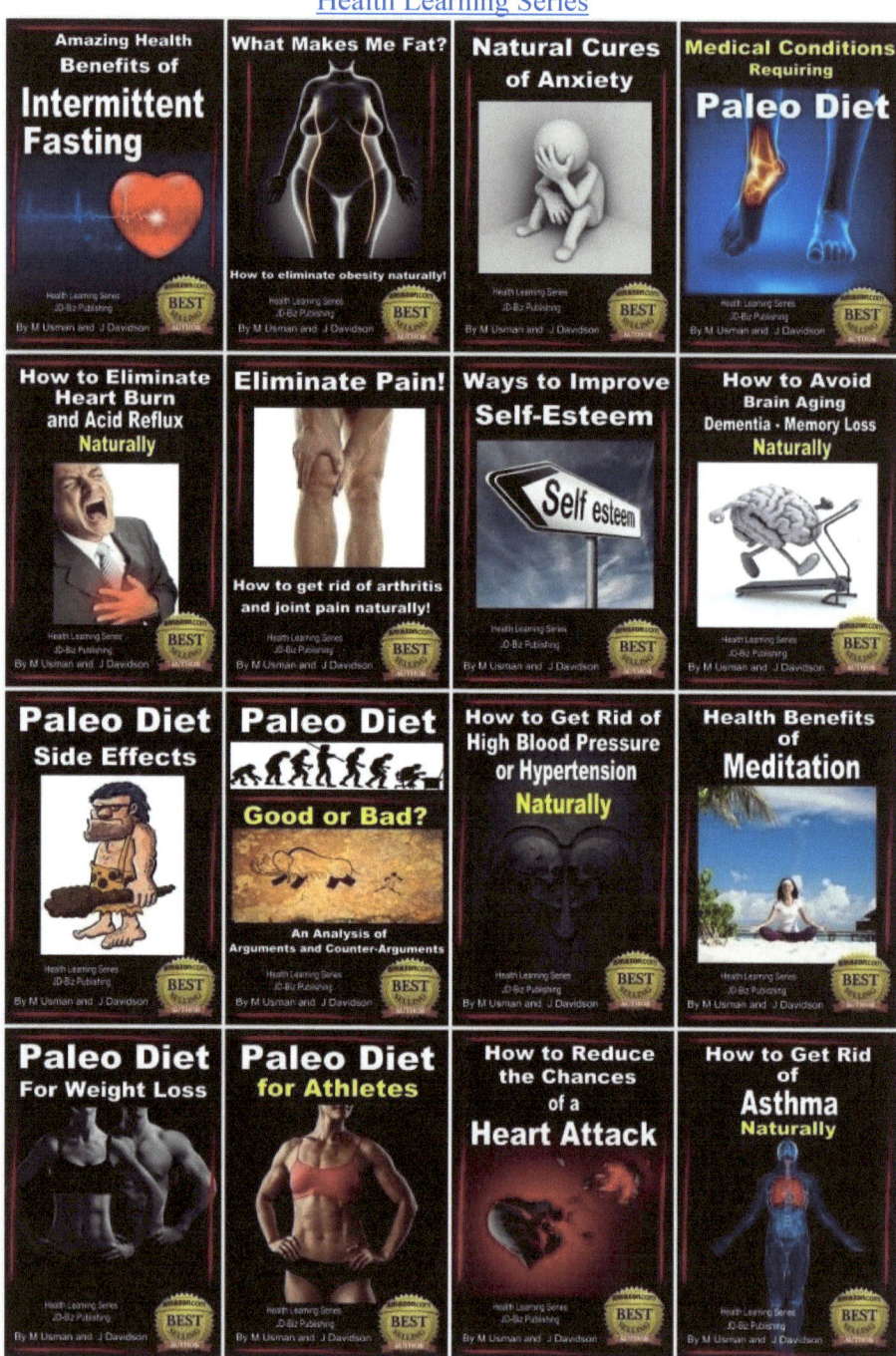

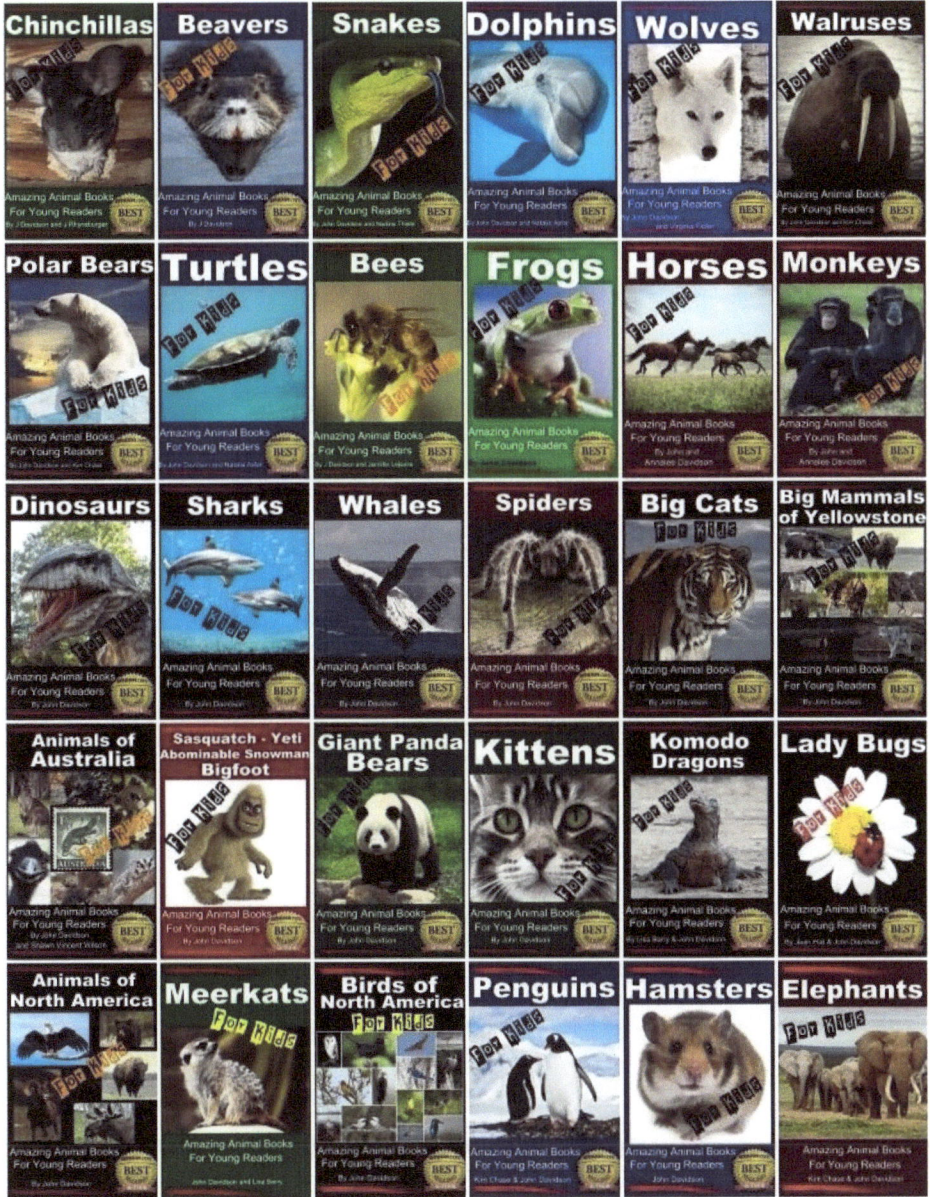

Learn To Draw Series

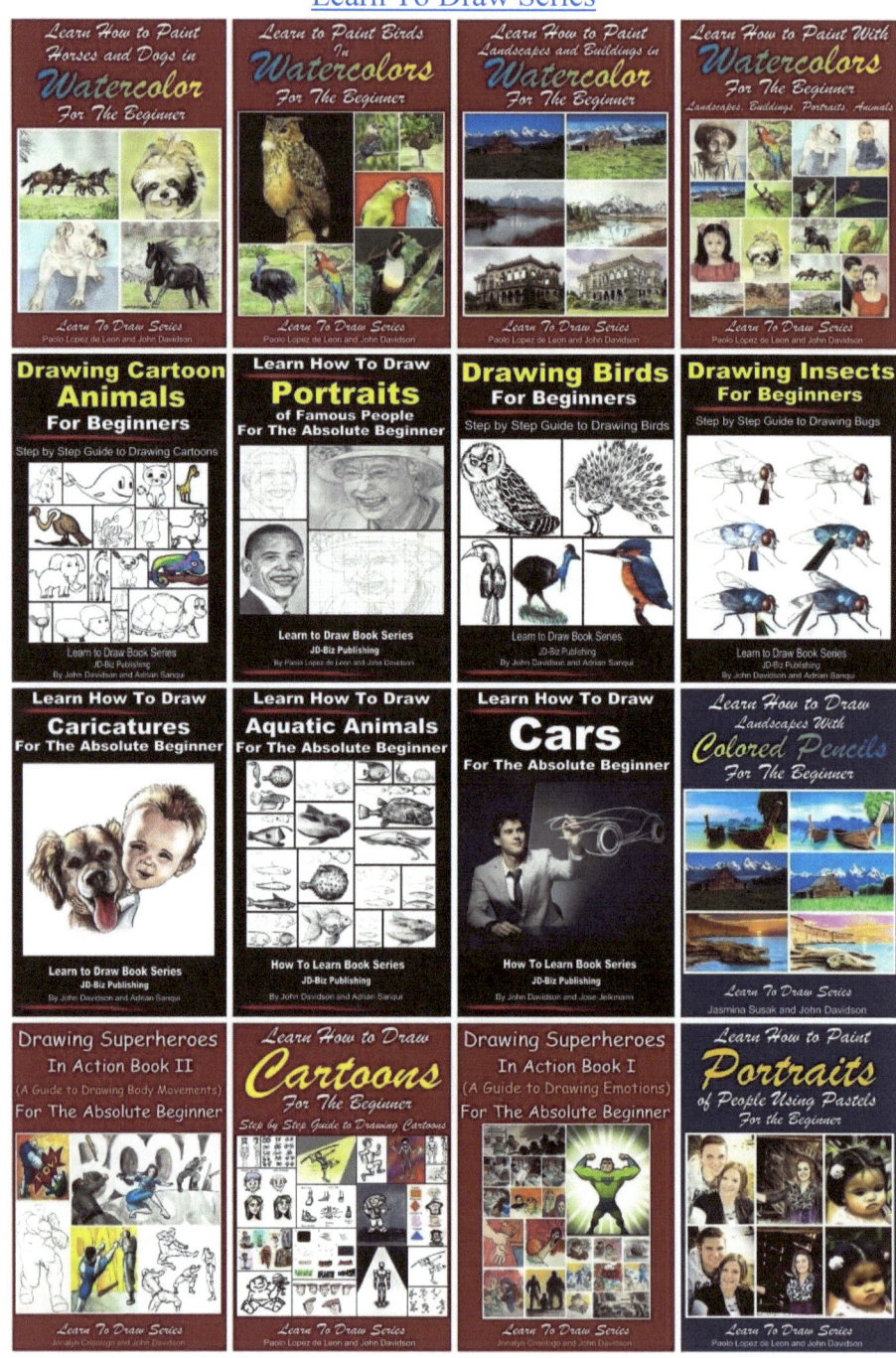

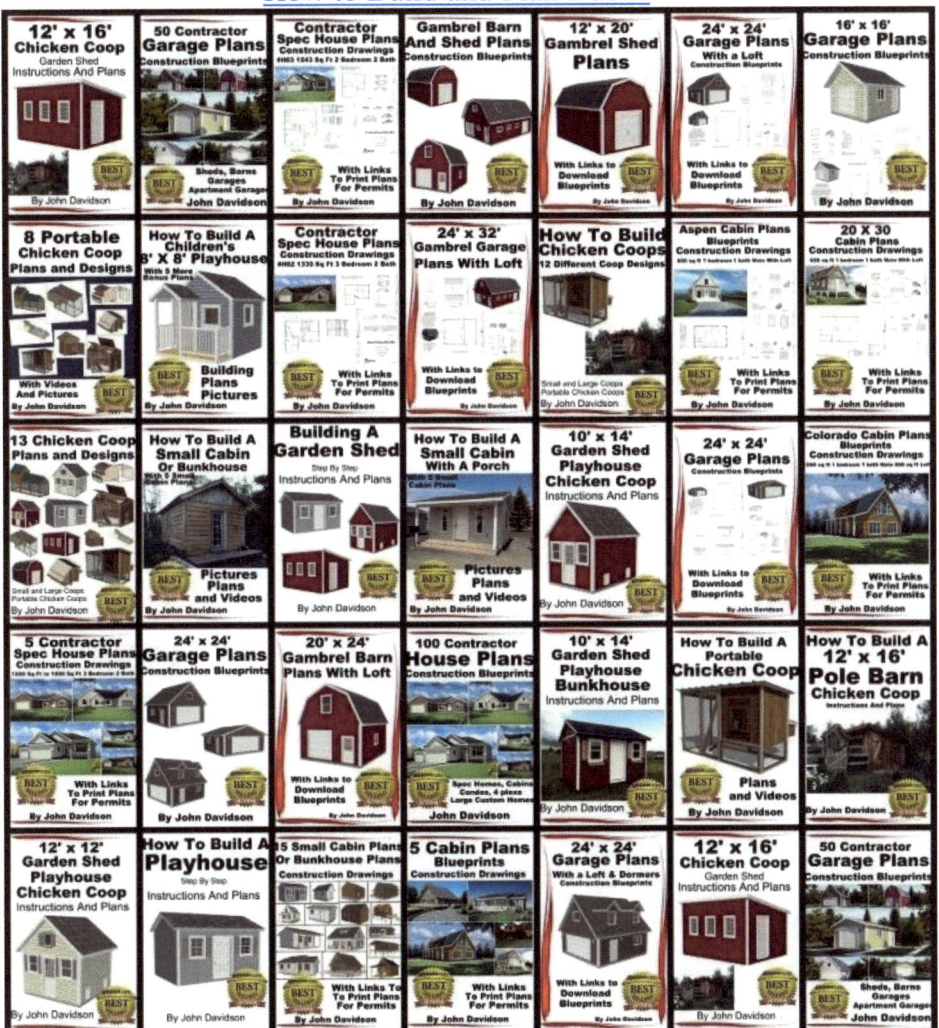

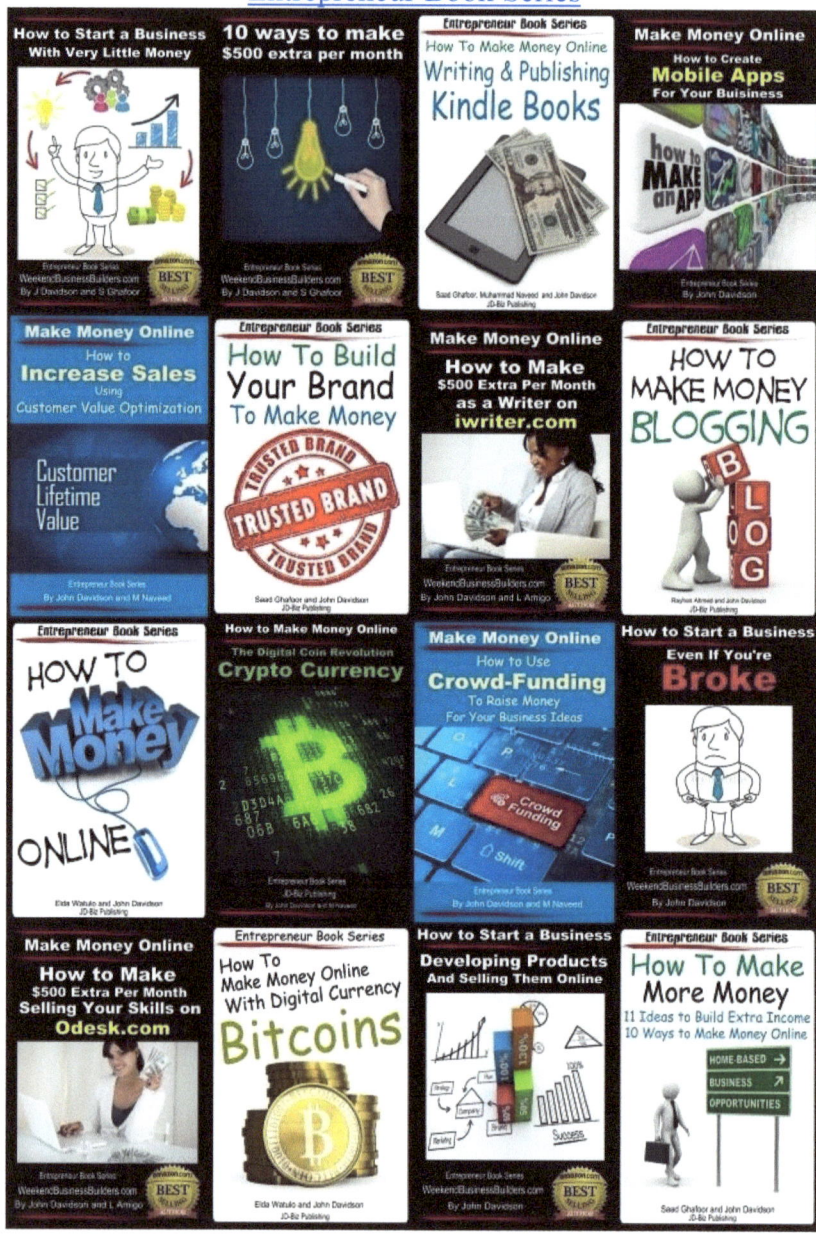

Our books are available at

1. Amazon.com

2. Barnes and Noble

3. Itunes

4. Kobo

5. Smashwords

6. Google Play Books

Download Free Books!
http://MendonCottageBooks.com

Publisher

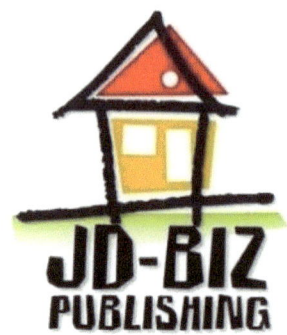

JD-Biz Corp

P O Box 374

Mendon, Utah 84325

http://www.jd-biz.com/

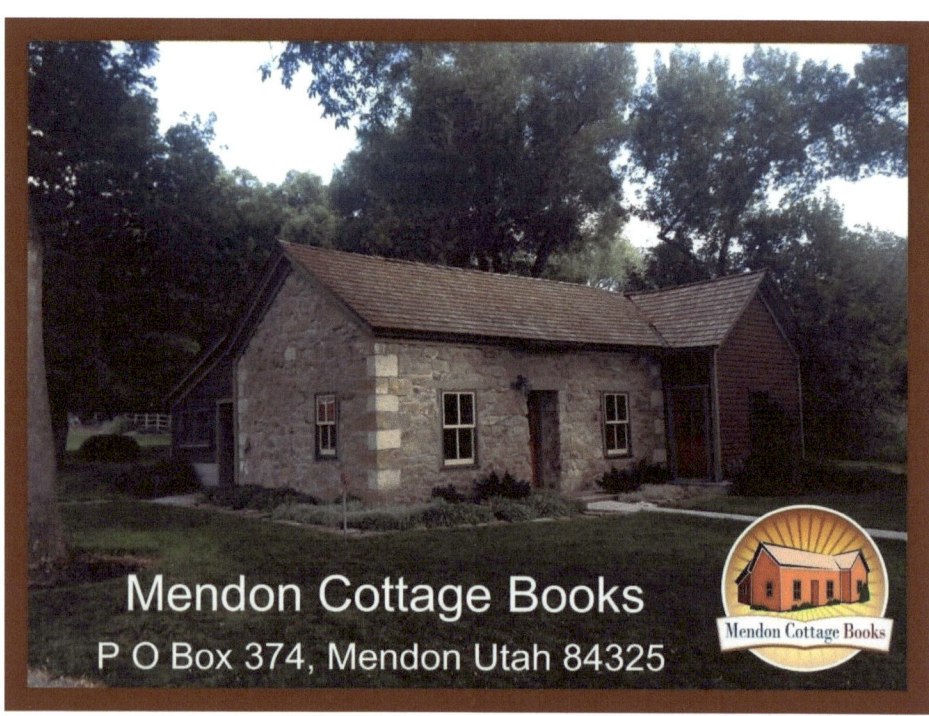